THE QUEST OF
PERSEUS

by Paul Collins
illustrated by Chris Burns

EDUCATORS PUBLISHING SERVICE
Cambridge and Toronto

© 2008 by Educators Publishing Service, a division of School Specialty Publishing, a member of the School Specialty Family

Series Authors: Kay Kovalevs and Alison Dewsbury
Commissioning Editors: Rachel Elliott, Tom Beran, Lynn Robbins, and Laura Woollett
Project managed by Rebecca Henson and Katherine Steward
Text by Paul Collins
Illustrated by Chris Burns
Edited by Emma Short
Designed by Justin Lim

Making Connections® developed by Educators Publishing Service, a division of School Specialty Publishing, and Pearson Education Australia, a division of Pearson Australia Group Pty Ltd.

ISBN 978 0 8388 3355 1

1 2 3 4 5 PEA 12 11 10 09 08

Printed in China.

CAST OF CHARACTERS

KING ACRISIUS (a-CRIS-e-us)
Grandfather of Perseus and king of Argos in Greece

ATHENA (a-THEE-na)
The goddess of wisdom

DANAË (DAN-a-ee)
Mother of Perseus, daughter of King Acrisius

DICTYS (DIK-tis)
A fisherman on the island of Seriphos

THE THREE GRAY WOMEN
Three old women who share one eye

HERMES (HER-meez)
The messenger god with winged sandals

THE KING OF SERIPHOS (SEH-ree-foss)
The cruel ruler of the island of Seriphos who wishes to marry Danaë

MEDUSA (me-DOO-sa)
An evil creature who can turn people to stone by looking at them

PERSEUS (PER-see-us)
A Greek hero who is the son of the god Zeus and of the woman Danaë

THE ANCIENT GREEKS BELIEVED THAT ORACLES COULD PREDICT THE FUTURE. ONE DAY, AN ORACLE TOLD KING ACRISIUS OF ARGOS THAT HIS GRANDSON, PERSEUS, WOULD KILL HIM. THIS PREDICTION FRIGHTENED THE KING. HE KNEW THAT HE MUST GET RID OF PERSEUS OR LIVE IN CONSTANT FEAR. KING ACRISIUS THOUGHT OF A WAY OUT. HE TRAPPED PERSEUS AND HIS MOTHER, DANAË, IN A WOODEN CRATE AND THREW THEM IN THE OCEAN. SURELY THEY WOULD DIE AT SEA. THEN THE KING WOULD NOT HAVE TO DO THE EVIL DEED HIMSELF.

THE EVIL MEDUSA FLEW AT PERSEUS.
SHE LET OUT A BLOOD-CURDLING WAIL.

25

THE PEOPLE OF SERIPHOS WANTED PERSEUS TO BE THEIR NEW KING. BUT PERSEUS WANTED TO RETURN TO ARGOS TO MAKE PEACE WITH HIS GRANDFATHER, KING ACRISIUS.

AND SO, PERSEUS AND DANAË SAILED FOR ARGOS.

You made a wise choice, Perseus. Dictys will be a fair king.

I hope Grandfather is half as fair. I don't know what we'll do if he still believes the oracle's prediction.

WHEN THEY ARRIVED, A CROWD MET THEM ON THE DOCK. EVERYONE WANTED TO SEE THE HERO WHO HAD DEFEATED THE KING OF SERIPHOS.

KING ACRISIUS HEARD THAT HIS GRANDSON HAD RETURNED. BUT HE WAS STILL AFRAID THAT PERSEUS WOULD KILL HIM. SO KING ACRISIUS DISGUISED HIMSELF AS A BEGGAR AND SLIPPED AWAY.

I don't understand it. Grandfather is gone.

I'm sorry, Perseus. I hoped he would have forgotten the oracle's prediction by now. But look, the people love you!

PERSEUS DIED MANY YEARS LATER. TO REWARD HIM FOR HIS HEROIC DEEDS, THE GODS MADE HIM IMMORTAL. THEY PLACED HIM IN THE NIGHT SKY AS A CONSTELLATION. YOU CAN STILL SEE HIM THERE TODAY, WITH HIS SWORD IN ONE HAND AND MEDUSA'S HEAD IN THE OTHER.